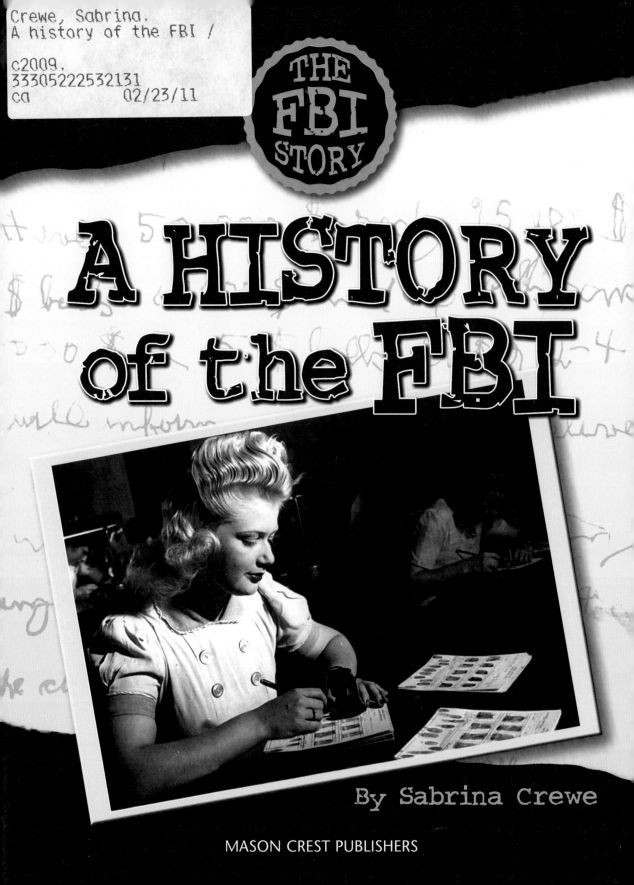

THE FBI STORY

A HISTORY of the FBI

By Sabrina Crewe

MASON CREST PUBLISHERS

Produced by OTTN Publishing in association with Water Buffalo Books.
Design by Westgraphix LLC.

MASON CREST PUBLISHERS INC.
370 Reed Road
Broomall, Pennsylvania 19008
(866) MCP-BOOK (toll free)
www.masoncrest.com

Printed in the United States of America

First Printing

9 8 7 6 5 4 3 2 1

Library of Congress Cataloging-in-Publication Data

Crewe, Sabrina.
        A history of the FBI / Sabrina Crewe.
            p. cm. — (FBI story)
        Includes bibliographical references and index.
        ISBN 978-1-4222-0563-1 (hardcover) — ISBN 978-1-4222-1377-3 (pbk.)
    1. United States. Federal Bureau of Investigation--Juvenile literature.
    2. Criminal investigation--United States--Juvenile literature. I. Title.
    HV8144.F43C74 2009
    363.250973--dc22   2008037494

Publisher's note:
All quotations in this book come from original sources and contain the spelling and
grammatical inconsistencies of the original text.

CONTENTS

CHAPTER 1 On the Trail

In 1934, Clyde Barrow and Bonnie Parker had been on the run for two years. During those two years, they stole cars and robbed banks. They were wanted for kidnapping and murder.

Bank robbers
Bonnie Parker and Clyde Barrow posed
for the photo above and the photo on the opposite page during
their 1932–1934 crime spree. The two invented a playful image
for themselves but were in fact ruthless killers.

Crime Spree

Bonnie and Clyde, as the famous couple is known, met in Texas in 1930. Clyde was sent to jail shortly afterward. In 1932, Bonnie smuggled him a gun. He used it to escape, and the two began their life of crime together. Kidnapping in Louisiana, stolen cars in Texas, and dead bodies everywhere—Bonnie and Clyde left a bloody trail across the United States.

For a while, Bonnie and Clyde formed a gang with three other people—Clyde Barrow's brother Buck; Buck's wife, Blanche; and William Daniel Jones. The gang of outlaws robbed many banks together. In 1933, however, Buck was killed in a shoot-out with police. Blanche Barrow and Jones were captured.

Bonnie and Clyde continued their killing spree. Their exploits made them famous. Every day, U.S. citizens tracked the **fugitives**' story in newspaper reports. Local law enforcement officers from New Mexico to Louisiana were on the case. There were many reported sightings of Bonnie and Clyde. In one documented sighting, the pair avoided capture by a sheriff and his deputies in Texas. In another, they released five prisoners in a daring raid on a Texas prison farm. It seemed as if they could never be caught.

5

This Wanted poster
for Bonnie and Clyde was issued in 1934
by the Division of Investigation (now called the FBI). It warned
arresting officers to use "extreme caution," as Bonnie and Clyde
were "wanted in connection with assault and murder of officers."

Special Agents

In addition to local law enforcement officers, however, another
force was on the trail. Agents from the Bureau of Investigation
were working day and night to track the criminals. These
agents were from a special team inside the U.S. government.
They got involved in the case in 1932, when a car stolen in
one state was found in another state. This kind of interstate
crime called for the Bureau's special agents.

The Bureau of Investigation issued Wanted posters with
photos of the criminals. They sent copies of Bonnie and

Clyde's fingerprints to local law enforcement agencies. Bureau agents went from state to state, following every lead.

Showdown

The trail of clues led agents to Louisiana, where Bonnie and Clyde had friends. In Louisiana, the Bureau of Investigation continued the hunt. An agent in the town of Ruston got word that the couple was nearby. Working with local law enforcement, Bureau of Investigation agents made a plan to trap Bonnie and Clyde.

Early in the morning of May 23, 1934, police officers hid in bushes along a road where Bonnie and Clyde were expected. They had put up a road-block to stop the couple's car. When they realized they were being

THE NAME AND THE MOTTO

The FBI's name changed a few times after it was founded in 1908. Its first name was "Bureau of Investigation." In 1932 it became the "United States Bureau of Investigation." This name changed to "Division of Investigation" just a year later. Not until 1935 did the agency get its current name: the Federal Bureau of Investigation.

That year, Inspector W. H. Drane Lester was editor of the FBI's employee magazine, *The Investigator*. He wrote:

At last we have a name that lends itself to dignified abbreviation: the Federal Bureau of Investigation, which quite naturally becomes "F B I." . . . "FBI" is the best and one from which we might well choose our motto, for those initials also represent the three things for which the Bureau and its representatives always stand: "Fidelity – Bravery – Integrity."

Because of Drane's comments, the FBI got a new motto along with its name. This motto—Fidelity, Bravery, Integrity—is displayed on the seal of the FBI. The seal also includes 13 gold stars, which stand for the original 13 states. The laurel branches have 46 leaves because there were 46 states when the FBI was founded. The FBI says the seal's blue color represents justice. The red stripes are for courage and strength, while the white stripes stand for truth and peace.

The J. Edgar Hoover Building, located in Washington, D.C., is the head-quarters of the FBI. It was named for the Bureau's most famous director.

ambushed, Bonnie and Clyde tried to escape. Driving away at top speed, they were caught in a shower of bullets. The car veered off the road. Bonnie and Clyde were both dead.

The FBI

The Bureau of Investigation is now the Federal Bureau of Investigation, or FBI. Bonnie and Clyde were just two of many famous criminals who have been tracked by FBI agents. The Bureau of Investigation is now called the Federal Bureau of Investigation, or FBI. Bonnie and Clyde were just two of the many famous criminals who have been tracked by its agents. Founded in 1908, the Bureau was charged with investigating federal crimes. A federal crime is one that crosses state borders or breaks the laws of the nation (as opposed to state laws). Over the years, the role of the FBI has grown.

Today, its stated mission is as follows:

> To protect and defend the United States against terrorist and foreign **intelligence** threats, to uphold and enforce the criminal laws of the United States, and to provide leadership and criminal justice services to federal, state, municipal, and international agencies and partners.

During its 100-year history, the FBI has investigated countless crimes. It has become a powerful force in the nation and abroad.

The FBI investigates many different types of federal crimes. Here, FBI agents remove materials from the home of a man suspected of selling information about secret U.S. technology to China.

2 The Early Days: Creating the FBI

Before 1908, the United States did not have its own force of special agents. If it needed to investigate a crime, the Department of Justice hired private detectives or used Secret Service agents from the Treasury Department. In 1908, in fact, the Department of Justice itself was fairly new. The government had created the department just a few decades before, in 1870.

New Laws

For most of the nation's history, law enforcement had been taken care of locally in each state. The federal government's job was to protect the nation from outside attack and encourage its growth. But as the nation grew, things

President Theodore Roosevelt's opposition to corruption fueled his desire to create a program to clean up illegal business practices.

changed. Businesses were getting bigger, and railroads were carrying people across the country.

The government introduced new laws to regulate large businesses and control expansion into new lands. It had to employ many expensive attorneys to look after all its legal work. So in 1870, Congress created the Department of Justice to handle the nation's legal business and enforce its new laws.

In 1908, Attorney General Charles J. Bonaparte hired a team of special agents to investigate crimes for the U.S. Department of Justice. That team formed a group that would one day become known as the FBI.

Investigators Wanted

The U.S. attorney general was (and still is) head of the Justice Department. From 1906 to 1909, the U.S. attorney general was a man named Charles J. Bonaparte. President Theodore Roosevelt told Bonaparte he needed to do something about land fraud (dishonestly taking land) and other crimes in the West.

Bonaparte saw the need for a unit of investigators to work in his department. In 1907, he asked Congress for some money for a small detective force, but Congress refused. And in 1908, Congress said that the Justice Department could no longer use Secret Service agents for its work. Now Bonaparte had even fewer resources to investigate crimes. He asked again if Congress would fund investigators for his department. Once more, Congress refused.

PINKERTON NATIONAL DETECTIVE AGENCY

In its early years, the Department of Justice often used private detectives to investigate crimes. The most legendary of these detectives was Allan Pinkerton, who started the Pinkerton National Detective Agency in 1850. Pinkerton agents performed investigations all over the United States. In 1861, Pinkerton discovered a plot to kill President Abraham Lincoln. For years, Pinkerton agents pursued famous outlaws in the West.

Much of Pinkerton's work came from big businesses. Pinkerton detectives worked first for railroad companies and banks. Large industrial companies began to employ the detectives as spies among their workers. Pinkerton agents would be called in to prevent workers from striking (stopping work to protest low wages or bad working conditions). In 1892, Pinkerton men shot and killed workers who had been locked out of their jobs at the Homestead steel plant in Pennsylvania. Afterward, Congress ordered the Department of Justice to stop employing Pinkerton agents.

A Team of Special Agents

On June 29, 1908, Bonaparte took matters into his own hands. He hired a team of agents for the Justice Department, paying for them out of a general expense fund.

In 1892, 10 people were killed in a violent clash between steelworkers and Pinkerton agents at the Homestead steel mill in Pennsylvania. The incident led the U.S. government to stop using Pinkerton detectives in federal investigations.

Bonaparte later explained his actions in a letter to President Roosevelt. He wrote:

> It became impossible for this Department to avail itself of the services of the Secret Service at all after July 1, 1908. . . . It became, therefore, unavoidable for the Department to itself organize a corps of special agents, and this it did. . . .

On July 26, 1908, Stanley W. Finch, chief examiner of the Department of Justice, became head of the group. In a founding order issued that day, the U.S. attorney general stated that "investigations under the Department . . . will be referred to the Chief Examiner" and his "force of special agents." Because of this order, the FBI marks July 26 as the date it was created.

By the end of 1908, the team had 34 members, many of them former private detectives or Secret Service agents. At first, the group of special agents had no name. In 1909, however, Bonaparte handed his office over to George Wickersham. On March 16, 1909, Wickersham named his team of investigators. He called it "the Bureau of Investigation." Stanley W. Finch became chief of the Bureau.

Getting Started

Before he left office, Bonaparte defined the role of the special agents. Their investigations would uncover crimes against the United States. These crimes would include those to do with banking, postal services, and

THEN AND NOW

The FBI was founded with 34 agents and no other employees. By 1958, there were 6,147 FBI agents supported by 7,839 other staff. In 2008, the FBI had 30,341 employees—12,590 special agents and 17,751 support staff.

When it was created, the FBI had its headquarters in Washington, D.C., and two field offices: one in New York City and one in Chicago. The FBI now has 56 field offices in major U.S. cities. There are also about 400 smaller offices across the nation. In other countries, the FBI has Legal Attaché offices, known as Legats. These offices are inside U.S. embassies in more than 70 cities around the world. Today, says FBI director Robert Mueller, "the globalization of crime . . . absolutely requires us to integrate law enforcement efforts around the world."

As the FBI has grown bigger, the organization has changed. Over the years, the agency has become more complex. It now has many divisions, as shown in this chart.

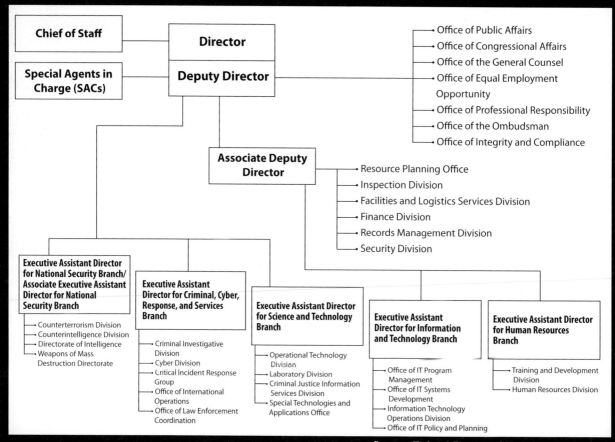

Source: Federal Bureau of Investigation

destruction of government property. The team would also look into serious crimes on Indian reservations. It would investigate land fraud in the newly settled West. Agents would also investigate companies suspected of breaking antitrust laws. These were laws that stopped big businesses from getting rid of all their competition.

Preventing Slavery

Some of the agents on the new team were already working for the Justice Department. They were investigators into the crime of peonage. Peonage forces people to work to pay off a debt, and it is seen as a form of slavery. The new team continued to uncover and prosecute this crime.

FAST FACTS

The Bureau used the Mann Act to convict **Ku Klux Klan** leader Edward Y. Clarke. Agents had no **evidence** to connect him with Klan activities. But in 1923, Clarke was charged with taking a woman from Texas to Louisiana for immoral purposes.

The Ku Klux Klan used violence as part of its campaign against African Americans, Jews, and other racial and religious minorities. The Bureau targeted the Klan in its efforts to combat domestic terrorism.

THE COMMUNIST THREAT

The U.S. government once believed that American **radicals** were influenced by communists from Russia. Communists are people who believe that all property and business in a country should be controlled by the state on behalf of the people. During World War I, the government of Russia was overthrown. Eventually the Russian Empire was replaced by the Soviet Union, a communist state.

To some Americans, communism seemed to offer a just society for working people. Communist ideas scared most Americans, however. They believed communism was a threat to their freedom and way of life. These fears fueled the actions of Bureau leaders and agents in the years following World War I and for many years to come.

In 1910, the Bureau became involved in another type of slavery. Many people worried that girls and young women were being taken from rural areas to big cities, where they were forced to become prostitutes. Congress passed a law named the White Slave Traffic Act, also known as the Mann Act. The law made it illegal to transport women across state lines for "immoral purposes." Soon, Bureau agents were sent to large cities all over the country to find victims and criminals under the Mann Act.

Foreign Enemies

In 1914, events in other countries led to a big change in the Bureau's role. That year, fighting broke out among nations in Europe—World War I had begun. The United States did not enter the war at first. But Americans were worried that foreign agents would commit **espionage** (spying to steal government secrets). They worried that foreigners would even persuade other Americans to harm their own country with **sabotage** (destructive actions).

In 1917, the United States entered World War I. That same year, Congress passed the Espionage Act. The act gave the Bureau many new powers. Agents began to investigate individuals they believed could harm the United States. They focused on "enemy **aliens**"—which at the time referred almost entirely to Germans living in the United States.

FAST FACTS

The General Intelligence Division (GID) was headed by a Justice Department attorney, J. Edgar Hoover. A few years later, Hoover would become head of the Bureau.

Target: Radicals

After World War I ended, the Bureau of Investigation's powers continued to grow. The Motor Vehicle Theft Act of 1919 (also called the Dyer Act) gave agents even more power to pursue criminals across state borders. The Bureau did not lose interest in enemies of the nation, however. After the war, the focus moved away from German spies. Instead, agents arrested labor union members and members of progressive organizations. The government believed many of these people to

[PLOT ALLEY]

YOU'RE ALL RIGHT!

AGITATION WHICH DELAYS OUR WAR INDUSTRIES IS "MADE IN GERMANY"

In the first seven months after America's entrance into this war for human freedom, enemy agitators in our midst caused 283,402 workers to lose 6,285,519 days of production. Our war industries were heavily handicapped by this unpatriotic strife.

LET US ALL PULL TOGETHER TO WIN THE WAR QUICKLY

Posters and cartoons warned Americans of German espionage agents and agitators working in the United States during World War I.

be radicals—people with strong ideas about changing society. The Bureau worked with another Justice Department unit that was created in 1919 just to collect information about radicals. The unit was named the General Intelligence Division (GID).

Stepping Over the Line

The Bureau and the GID collected thousands of documents about people and organizations. Bureau agents raided labor union offices. They worked with immigration officials to deport immigrants from other nations who had radical ideas.

Russian-born U.S. citizen Emma Goldman was involved in a variety of radical causes, including an effort to convince American men to resist being drafted into the army during World War I. J. Edgar Hoover, head of the GID, took the lead in having her deported in 1919.

In January 1920, the Bureau of Investigation and Bureau of Immigration rounded up 10,000 Communist Party members and followers. These roundups were called the Palmer Raids. They were named after Attorney General A. Mitchell Palmer, who had ordered them.

The arrests were at first viewed favorably by the press and by most of the public. One *New York Times* headline proclaimed: "Revolution Smashed." Soon, however, people realized that the Bureau had stepped over the line. Many people had been arrested and detained without charge. Most of these people had committed no crime and posed no threat to the nation.

Many of the orders to deport immigrants were overturned by court and government officials. Only about 250 people actually left the country. A government inquiry said that Palmer had used the power of his office unfairly against people he considered enemies of the United States. The inquiry found that Palmer had abused his power as attorney general.

Time for Change

The Bureau continued to investigate political **activists**, however. It also tried to find information that would damage the reputations of two U.S. senators, Burton Wheeler and Thomas Walsh. In 1923 and 1924, these senators looked into a suspicious oil deal that involved a powerful government official, Secretary of the Interior Albert Fall. The government found out that the Bureau was again abusing its powers. This time, it was to help Fall cover up his dishonesty. As a consequence of this attempted cover-up, Attorney General Harry Daugherty had to resign in April 1924. In May, Bureau director William J. Burns was fired. It was time for a new leader.

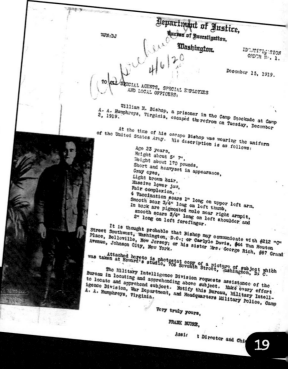

"Identification Order Number 1," for William N. Bishop, an escaped military prisoner, was the Bureau's first Wanted poster. It appeared in 1919.

CHAPTER 3 Hoover in Charge: Reform and Growth

In 1924, people did not think much of the Bureau of Investigation. There had been scandals and abuses of power. Top officials in the Justice Department had been fired because of their actions.

New Men at the Top

A new U.S. attorney general, Harlan F. Stone, wanted to restore public confidence. He shut down the GID and said the era of spying on radicals was over. From now on, said Stone, the Bureau would not concern itself with "political or other opinions of individuals . . . only with their conduct and then only with such conduct as is forbidden by the laws of the United States." In other words, people's beliefs were their own business. The Bureau's business was to enforce laws.

J. Edgar Hoover became head of the Bureau in 1924, at the age of 29. He remained FBI director until his death in 1972.

On May 10, 1924, the U.S. attorney general appointed J. Edgar Hoover to lead the Bureau of Investigation. Hoover's job was to reform the Bureau and make it more professional.

Lower Costs, Higher Standards

In May 1924, the Bureau had 650 employees and more than 50 field offices. By the end of the year, Hoover had fired 62 employees and shut down five of the offices. He continued to reduce the number of staff and field offices over the next five years.

With new leadership, Bureau agents became better trained. Their conduct improved under Hoover's strict eye. Hoover took some important steps to make the Bureau more professional.

JOHN EDGAR HOOVER
(JANUARY 1, 1895–MAY 2, 1972)

Hoover was born and raised in Washington, D.C. When he finished high school, he got a job at the Library of Congress. At night, he went to law school. Hoover received his degree in 1917 and went to work in the Department of Justice. First he investigated enemy aliens. Then, as head of the new General Intelligence Division, Hoover gathered information about radicals.

Hoover became director of the Bureau in 1924 at the age of 29. His personal beliefs had a great impact on the FBI's actions. Hoover carried on a lifelong crusade against people he believed were a threat to the nation. He pursued gangsters in the 1930s and enemy aliens in the 1940s. In the 1950s, the FBI focused on communists—to Hoover, they were the biggest evil of all. Civil rights leaders, especially Martin Luther King Jr., became Hoover's targets in the 1960s.

Hoover secretly collected information about government officials and other public figures. He became a very powerful figure himself and was both feared and respected. Presidents and attorneys general came and went, but Hoover stayed in office. President Lyndon Johnson even changed the rules for Hoover. In 1964, he issued a special order that allowed Hoover to stay in office after the retirement age of 70. At the time of his death in 1972, Hoover had been leading the FBI for almost half a century.

These steps included the following:

- Setting up the Fingerprints Division in Washington, D.C., as a central repository for fingerprints collected throughout the country (1924).
- Opening a training school for new agents (1928).
- Creating the Bureau's Crime Laboratory (1932).

Hoover also helped train other law enforcers. In 1935, the FBI National Academy began teaching state and local police officers. It was Hoover's goal to set a national standard for fighting crime.

Winning Respect

Hoover knew that the Bureau needed the respect of the American people to do a good job. He wanted agents to have a good public image. In 1925, Hoover wrote to the U.S. attorney general:

> The Agents of the Bureau of Investigation have been impressed with the fact that the real problem of law enforcement is in trying to obtain the cooperation and sympathy of the public and that they cannot hope to get such cooperation until they themselves merit the respect of the public.

Hoover's high standards helped achieve this respect. Other factors helped, too. By the early 1930s, it seemed as if a crime wave was sweeping the nation. This period, known as the gangster era, was a time when people were afraid that local law officers could not deal with violent crime gangs. Some of these gangs, like Bonnie and Clyde's Barrow gang, were relatively small and mostly robbed banks and businesses. Others operated on a larger scale. These gangs controlled large sums of money and ran illegal businesses, including prostitution and the sale of illegal drugs and alcohol. These gangs had bosses who oversaw the gang's activities. They also hired people to enforce the gang's rules, collect money, intimidate ordinary business-people, and kill rival gangsters.

FAST FACTS

On October 11, 1925, agent Edwin C. Shanahan was killed while trying to arrest a car thief. He was the first Bureau agent killed on the job.

Agents in the Headlines

Investigating crimes such as murder and robbery was not part of the Bureau's job, and for decades Hoover did not show much interest in taking on organized crime. When killers and thieves crossed state borders, however, Hoover's team showed up. In the 1930s, the Bureau was involved in several high-profile cases. Bureau agents gained a reputation as successful crime-fighters.

One case involved the 1932 kidnap and murder of a 20-month-old child.

The Bureau was brought in to investigate the 1932 kidnapping of the son of famed aviator Charles Lindbergh and writer Anne Morrow Lindbergh.

G-MEN

FBI agents acquired a popular public image in the 1930s. They became known as "G-men," short for "Government Men." Some people believe the nickname was born during the capture of a famous gangster, George "Machine Gun" Kelly. In 1933, agents surrounded a house where Kelly was staying. FBI historian John Fox told the story in a radio interview in June 2008:

> He was hiding out in a rooming house and when we entered, as legend has it, he threw up his hands and shouted, "Don't shoot G-men, don't shoot." . . . Whether or not Kelly actually said something like that, chances are he probably didn't, but it was a legend that caught on.

The G-man, people believed, "always gets his man." In books and on the radio, in movies and on television, G-men were celebrated as heroes. Children joined Junior G-men clubs and read G-men comic books. *Gang Busters*, an FBI radio show, ran for more than 20 years.

FBI director J. Edgar Hoover was personally responsible for some of this fame and glamour. He put pressure on movie-makers to make special agents—not gangsters—the stars of their movies. For years, Hollywood kept the G-man image alive.

Today's movies offer a different image of the FBI. The *Miss Congeniality* movies of 2000 and 2005 were comedies. They followed the activities of a female **undercover** FBI agent. *The Kingdom* (2007), starring Jamie Foxx, reflects current fears. It shows FBI agents working to find terrorists in the Middle East.

He was the son of pilot Charles Lindbergh and writer Anne Morrow Lindbergh. The case got a huge amount of attention. President Herbert Hoover said the Bureau of Investigation would join the hunt for the killer. Through a series of clues, the Bureau traced the crime to Bruno Richard Hauptmann, who was executed in 1936.

Another case gained fame for the Bureau at about the same time. John Dillinger was a famous bank robber. Hoover gave him a special nickname: "Public Enemy Number One." Dillinger and his gang had often escaped capture by state and local police. In 1934, Dillinger escaped from jail in Indiana and took off in a sheriff's car to Illinois. He had crossed a state line in a stolen car, which was a federal crime. The Bureau entered the chase. Following a tip from a female companion, agents cornered Dillinger at the Biograph movie theater in Chicago. He was killed as he tried to escape.

John Dillinger's face was plastered across newspapers and Wanted posters between the time of his escape from prison and his death at the hands of federal agents in 1934.

The Kansas City Massacre

On June 17, 1933, police and Bureau agents arrived at Union Railway Station in Kansas City, Missouri, with

The aftermath of the Kansas City Massacre, in which four lawmen and their prisoner were killed in a failed attempt by gunmen to free the prisoner.

prisoner Frank Nash. Three gunmen—all of them notorious criminals—ambushed the group. Firing machine guns and pistols, they shot four of the seven lawmen and the prisoner.

The Bureau pursued the gunmen with all its resources. In October 1934, the manhunt ended in a shoot-out between Bureau agents and the outlaw Charles "Pretty Boy" Floyd. Floyd was killed. The violence of the Kansas City Massacre highlighted the dangerous nature of gangsters. It caused outrage among Americans. They were willing to accept an expanded role for federal law officers.

More Responsibilities

In the 1930s, the Bureau gained more power. People feared crime, and President Franklin D. Roosevelt pushed for new laws. These laws expanded the crime-fighting role of the U.S. government. Kidnapping became a federal crime if the victim was not found within seven days. Transporting stolen property was now a federal crime if state borders were crossed. Bank robbery also became a federal crime. So did racketeering and extortion (ways of getting money through illegal businesses or by threatening people). During this period, agents officially gained the right to carry guns and make arrests.

After 1935, the Bureau of Investigation was known as the Federal Bureau of Investigation, or FBI. The FBI's expanded role had an impact on violent crime. Most major gang leaders were caught (or killed) by the late 1930s.

Secret Intelligence Work

During the 1930s, other issues arose. It was the time of the Great Depression, when millions of people lost their jobs. Once again, there was political unrest. Government officials worried that certain political groups in the United States were **subversive**—that is, they wanted to undermine U.S. society or the U.S. government. Some of these groups might be a threat to national security by opening the door for foreign espionage. Fears of communism, and of the communist Soviet Union, lingered. But another concern had arisen as well. In Italy and Germany, fascism had taken root. Fascism is a political movement holding that individuals are less important than the nation (or even a racial group). **Fascists** believe that society should be highly regimented, and that it is acceptable for the government to control every aspect of citizens' lives. Fascists also tend to believe that their country is superior

An investigator scans two sets of fingerprints for similarities. Over the years, the FBI has helped state and local law enforcement officials solve countless crimes through its vast database of fingerprints.

to other countries. Fascist states are ruled by dictators. In Germany, Adolf Hitler and the Nazis were in power. In Italy, it was Benito Mussolini and the Fascist Party.

During the 1930s, some Americans accepted the ideas of fascism. In 1936, President Roosevelt secretly requested that Hoover provide a "broad picture" of fascist and communist activities in the United States.

Hoover began a huge program to gather information, or intelligence. He looked for evidence of subversive activities in industries such as shipping and steel. The FBI examined the military and the nation's schools. Agents focused on labor union leaders and political activists.

This kind of intelligence gathering had gotten the Bureau into trouble earlier—in the years following World War I. The FBI's intelligence activities would now be kept secret. But they would also soon become its most crucial role. The threat of another war was looming over the world.

Dictators Benito Mussolini of Italy (left) and Adolf Hitler of Germany. During the 1930s, with World War II on the horizon, President Franklin D. Roosevelt directed the FBI to gather information about possible supporters of Mussolini and Hitler in the United States.

CHAPTER 4 Enemies at Home and Abroad: Spies and Politics

World War II began in September 1939, when Germany invaded Poland. Britain and France then declared war on Germany. The war soon spread across the globe. Germany, Italy, and Japan formed a coalition known as the Axis powers. They were opposed by nations known as the Allies. At the outset of the war, the largest of the Allies were Britain and France. The Soviet Union would join the Allies after Germany invaded it in June 1941.

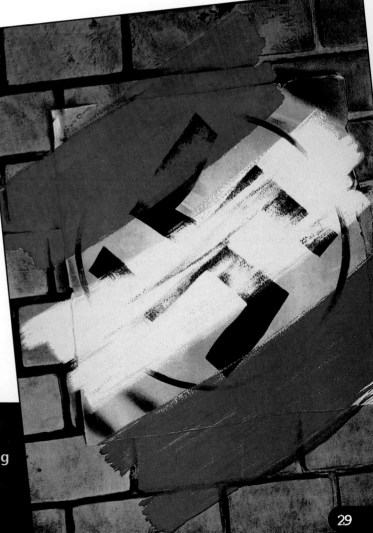

This World War II propaganda poster shows a swastika, the symbol of Nazi Germany, being obliterated by the red, white, and blue of the United States.

SPIES AND SABOTEURS

The FBI caught a number of spies and saboteurs during World War II. With the help of a **double agent**, the agency uncovered a large German spy ring in New York. A double agent is someone who pretends to work for one side while really working for the other. William Sebold was a German-born U.S. citizen who was recruited by Nazi Germany's secret police while on a visit to his native country. The Germans trained him to be a radio operator so he could send and receive information when he returned to the United States. Back in the United States, however, Sebold became a double agent for the FBI. Sebold operated his radio link while the FBI collected information. In 1941, the FBI arrested 33 spies who had sent military information to Germany.

In June 1942, Germany sent eight men in two submarines to the United States. Their mission was to destroy and disrupt important facilities, such as factories. The first team landed on Long Island on June 13. The team's leader, George John Dasch, soon lost his nerve and turned himself in. Meanwhile, the second submarine arrived in Florida. Dasch told the FBI where to find the other saboteurs. The other seven men were quickly arrested. Dasch's role was kept secret until after the war, so the FBI received full credit for capturing the saboteurs.

William Sebold was a German-born double agent working for the FBI. Here he is shown talking to Fritz Duquesne, the leader of a notorious Nazi spy ring. Unbeknownst to Duquesne, he was being filmed, and the evidence gathered from Sebold's work led to the arrest of Duquesne and the rest of his gang.

Expanded Role

During the first two and a half years of the war, the United States remained officially neutral. Many Americans wanted it that way. Many others thought the United States should help nations resist aggression by Italy and, especially, Nazi Germany.

Agents of the Special Intelligence Service (SIS), a branch of the FBI developed to do counterintelligence work against enemies of the Allied cause during World War II.

Behind America's official neutrality, President Franklin D. Roosevelt was actually supporting the Allies in important ways. For example, the United States provided massive amounts of aid—in the form of military equipment and money—to Britain and other Allied countries. This, of course, did not please Axis powers Germany, Italy, and Japan.

Roosevelt put the FBI in charge of all counterespionage work. The FBI would be responsible for catching foreign spies and preventing sabotage. Privately, the president told Hoover to send agents to South America, where there were many supporters of fascism. Hoover created the Special Intelligence Service (SIS) in 1940 to do this.

By 1940, Congress had passed laws that gave the FBI authority to gain information about radicals of any sort in the United States. Some of these people, including communists

THE INTERNMENT CAMPS

Most of the people rounded up as likely enemy sympathizers during World War II were of Japanese descent. Most were ordinary people targeted on the basis of their ancestry, race, and appearance. Sadly, thousands of resident aliens and U.S. citizens alike were sent to camps where they lived for most of the war. When they were released from these camps—called internment camps—many of them had lost nearly all their possessions. All they had was what little they had been allowed to pack into their suitcases. It was only decades later that the government offered them some form of apology and compensation for being wrongfully detained during the war. By then, about half of the detainees had died.

FBI director J. Edgar Hoover opposed the internment of Japanese Americans. According to Hoover, the FBI had conducted its own investigation into possible enemy agents living among resident aliens and U.S. citizens. In a secret six-page memo to the U.S. attorney general, Hoover argued against the internments: "Every complaint in this regard has been investigated, but in no case has any information been obtained which would substantiate the allegation."

Despite Hoover's opposition to the arrests and internments, the Bureau complied with the government's orders to help round up and confine an estimated 120,000 Japanese Americans during the war.

and supporters of fascism, were believed to be threats to national security. But, following President Roosevelt's instructions, the FBI also monitored people who simply disagreed with the president's policies. Hoover kept secret lists of "potentially dangerous" people.

The Bureau engaged in several activities that were illegal. Agents used **wiretaps** to secretly listen to people's telephone conversations. Wire-

tapping was against the law. So was opening citizens' mail, but the FBI did that, too. Hoover allowed his agents to break other laws. They entered offices and houses to hide bugs (listening devices) and obtain information.

During the War

On December 7, 1941, Japan attacked the U.S. naval base in Pearl Harbor, Hawaii. The following day, the United States officially declared war on Japan. On December 11, Germany and Italy declared war on the United States. America was now fully committed to fighting in World War II on the side of the Allies.

On December 7, even before the official declaration of war against Japan, Roosevelt issued a presidential proclamation that affected many resident aliens (non-citizens) in the United States—and some U.S. citizens. After declaring that "an invasion has been perpetrated upon the territory of the United States by [the] Empire of Japan," Presidential Proclamation 2525 declared, "Alien enemies deemed dangerous to the public peace or safety of the United States by the Attorney General or the Secretary of War . . . are subject to summary apprehension [arrest]."

The FBI had already prepared a list of people who would be arrested in the event of war. Most were Japanese,

Most of the people of Japanese descent whom U.S. authorities rounded up and held in detention camps during World War II were U.S. citizens.

Italian, and German resident aliens. Some were U.S. citizens suspected of being sympathetic to the enemy. Agents immediately went to round up these people. Most of them were handed over to other authorities, such as the immigration service. Later, tens of thousands of Japanese Americans were sent to detention camps.

During World War II, the FBI's field offices operated 24 hours a day. Until the war was over, the Bureau focused on uncovering sabotage and capturing enemy agents. It also continued with its everyday criminal investigations.

The Enemy Within

As World War II drew to a close in 1945, the FBI's focus shifted once more onto Americans. The FBI was no longer the nation's coordinator for foreign intelligence. But it could use the techniques developed in wartime against suspected communists. The Soviet Union, once a U.S. ally in the war against Nazi Germany, was now the chief political and military rival of the United States. As a communist nation, it represented a special threat to what would become

In 1950 the FBI broke up a spy ring that passed U.S. atomic-weapons secrets to the Soviet Union. Among those arrested were a married couple, Julius and Ethel Rosenberg. The two New Yorkers were convicted of espionage and executed in 1953.

known as the American way of life. And now, more than ever, Hoover was afraid of communist influence within the United States.

In 1945, government employees became the subject of FBI investigations. There had been leaks of top-secret documents to the news media. The FBI found traitors among government staff. Bureau employees spent more and more time doing background checks both for the government and for non-government groups. Most of this side of the FBI's work was done in secret.

Hoover launched a huge campaign to persuade the public that

Charlie Chaplin, a British-born actor and movie director, achieved great success in Hollywood. But Chaplin left the United States in 1952, in part because he objected to the anti-communist hysteria in the country. The FBI investigated Chaplin but found no evidence that he had ever been a member of the Communist Party.

CELEBRITY BLACKLIST

In the period of anti-communist fears, the FBI and others believed that the Communist Party had gained a hold on the movie industry. Beginning in 1942, the FBI investigated Hollywood. A 1943 FBI memo stated that many actors and writers "appear to be under control and direction of the Communist Party." The memo also said, "Quite a number of directors and executives are well-known communists."

In 1947, actors, writers, and others were summoned to appear before the House Committee on Un-American Activities (HUAC) to be questioned about their activities. People suspected of being communists were blacklisted. This meant they could not work in their professions. In 1951, another round of HUAC hearings caused hundreds more to be blacklisted. HUAC investigated other professions, and more **blacklists** were created. Radio personalities, teachers, lawyers, and journalists lost their jobs. They were all denied employment because of their suspected beliefs.

communism was a dire threat to the nation. He also tried to fight communism with **counterintelligence**. The FBI would spread negative information about groups and individuals. It did what it could to divide and weaken political groups, especially the Communist Party. These counter-intelligence programs, or COINTELPROs, started in 1956 and ran into the early 1970s.

FAST FACTS

The FBI's "Ten Most Wanted Fugitives" list was first published on March 14, 1950. It circulated photos of the nation's most dangerous criminals.

Pursuing Communists

It wasn't just the FBI that was pursuing communists. Congress had a committee to investigate political activity. It was named the House Committee on Un-American Activities, or HUAC. The FBI would supply HUAC with information to use in its hearings. In 1947, HUAC announced it would investigate the movie industry. The FBI produced a list of Hollywood names.

For a while, Hoover had an ally in his anti-communist crusade. Wisconsin senator Joseph McCarthy declared in a 1950 speech that the government was full of communists:

> In my opinion the State Department, which is one of the most important government departments, is thoroughly infested with communists.

> I have in my hand fifty-seven cases of individuals who would appear to be either card-carrying members or certainly loyal to the Communist Party, but who nevertheless are still helping to shape our foreign policy.

One thing to remember in discussing the communists in our government is that we are not dealing with spies who get thirty pieces of silver to steal the blueprints of new weapons. We are dealing with a far more sinister type of activity because it permits the enemy to guide and shape our policy.

The nation was already gripped by a fear of communism. McCarthy's speech added fuel to the fire. With Hoover's help, McCarthy pursued suspected communists on college campuses. But in 1953, when McCarthy went after the military, his campaign of fear backfired. Televised hearings showed McCarthy as a cruel bully, and he quickly lost public support. Hoover soon distanced the FBI from the senator.

The Cold War Era

The climate of suspicion did not go away with McCarthy. It was the Cold War era, a time of hostility between the United States and the Soviet Union. The Cold War would last for many years, even if the panic had died down.

The FBI continued to investigate large numbers of people. Hoover's files on suspicious individuals kept growing. The Bureau did catch some Soviet agents working in the United States. With the help of undercover agents, the FBI gained entry into the American Communist Party. This undercover work gave FBI agents access to Soviet secrets. But the mood in the country was changing. Other issues would soon come under the FBI spotlight.

U.S. senator Joseph McCarthy targeted Hollywood, universities, and the military in his hunt for suspected communists in the early 1950s.

5 A Changing Nation: Civil Rights and Organized Crime

World War II and the Cold War that followed
caused the FBI to focus on intelligence work.
The Bureau's role in fighting crime also continued to grow.

MURDER, INC.

This 1940 police photograph shows three hit men who were members of a group
of contract killers nicknamed Murder, Inc., by the press. Murder, Inc.—set up
to enforce the rules of America's organized crime families—is believed to have
carried out at least 1,000 contract killings all over the country, mostly during
the 1930s. Despite this, FBI director J. Edgar Hoover long denied the existence
of a national network of criminal gangs.

A Web of Crime

The FBI knew that family-based networks controlled certain areas of crime. Organized groups in large cities ran gambling, prostitution, and the drug trade. But these illegal activities were not federal offenses, and Hoover said local law officers should deal with them. In 1957, however, it became clear that criminals from all parts of the country were working together. That year, a New York state trooper stumbled upon a meeting of crime bosses in the rural town of Apalachin. According to FBI historian John Fox, the meeting "did signal to the FBI that this was a national web and needed to be dealt with at a national level."

The crime networks or families were known as "the Mafia," a name that came from Italian criminal networks. "The Mob" was a simple nickname that many people used.

Changing the Law

Hoover created the Top Hoodlum program in 1957 to pursue crime leaders. It was a tough job. Hardly anyone would inform on the Mafia—doing so usually meant death—and undercover agents found it impossible to penetrate the Mob's ranks. Instead, the FBI used wiretaps and bugged

Mob headquarters. But because these methods were against the law, the information gathered could not be used to prosecute Mafia members.

In the early 1960s, U.S. attorney general Robert Kennedy asked Congress to change wiretapping laws. It took several years, but in 1968 and 1970, two new laws were passed that were very important to the FBI.

The first was the Omnibus Crime Control and Safe Streets (OCCSS) Act of 1968. It allowed for wiretaps and bugs to be used in investigations (with a court-approved warrant). This law made it much easier for the FBI to collect evidence against the Mob and other criminals.

In 1970, the Racketeer Influenced and Corrupt Organizations (RICO) law outlawed the use of a business for criminal activity. Businesses funded by crime money became illegal, too. RICO helped the FBI target criminal activities such as drug dealing, gambling, and **money laundering**.

Joseph Valachi was a member of a New York crime family who became an informer against the Mafia. In 1962 and 1963, he disclosed the inner workings of the crime network to the FBI. In 1968, a book based on his memoirs and interviews, called *The Valachi Papers,* became a best seller and the basis for a movie of the same name.

ASSASSINATION

The 1960s were marked by the assassinations of three nationally prominent public figures within a five-year period. In November 1963, President John F. Kennedy was killed during a public appearance in Dallas, Texas. The civil rights leader Martin Luther King Jr. was shot in April 1968 at his motel in Memphis, Tennessee. Two months later, the late president's brother, Senator Robert F. Kennedy—the former U.S. attorney general—was gunned down while campaigning in Los Angeles for the 1968 Democratic presidential nomination.

The FBI played a major role in investigating all three assassinations. Two days after Lee Harvey Oswald was arrested for killing President Kennedy, Oswald was shot by a man named Jack Ruby. President Lyndon Johnson told the FBI to investigate the shootings. It turned out that the FBI had twice before investigated Oswald for connections to the Soviet Union. Both the Bureau and the Warren Commission, which President Johnson had formed to investigate the Kennedy assassination, conducted thousands of interviews and concluded that Oswald had acted alone.

A 1979 report by Congress questioned the conclusions of the FBI and Warren Commission that Oswald had acted alone. The congressional report stated that certain evidence suggested the possibility of a **conspiracy** to kill Kennedy. In the years since then, however, no proof of a conspiracy has been uncovered.

More than 3,000 FBI agents worked to find the killer of Martin Luther King Jr. They identified James Earl Ray by the fingerprints on the murder weapon, a rifle. They then traced Ray to Canada and on to England, where he was arrested just a few weeks after the killing.

When Robert Kennedy was shot, his assailant was caught right away. The FBI spent many hours investigating the case anyway. Agents produced several thousand pages of reports. As with the two other killings, they did this to rule out the idea of a conspiracy.

Martin Luther King Jr. was the most prominent leader of the civil rights movement. King was assassinated in Memphis, Tennessee, on April 4, 1968. The FBI launched a massive investigation, and the killer, James Earl Ray, was captured in London in June 1968.

A police officer confronts a civil rights demonstrator in Nashville, Tennessee, 1964. While the campaign to secure equality for African Americans gained momentum during the 1960s, FBI director J. Edgar Hoover was trying to discredit leaders in the civil rights movement, especially Martin Luther King Jr., whom Hoover suspected of having ties with communists.

Social Change

Meanwhile, major changes were taking place in U.S. society. During the 1960s, the civil rights movement gained momentum. African Americans demanded an end to racially discriminatory laws and practices. Women, too, began to insist on equality with men. Young people questioned and protested government policies, especially U.S. involvement in the Vietnam War.

Hoover believed that many of the political and social movements of the 1960s threatened society. Under his leadership, the FBI expanded its counterintelligence programs. The FBI's COINTELPROs targeted people such as antiwar protesters and African American militants.

Hoover and Civil Rights

But Hoover was no supporter of the mainstream civil rights movement either. Behind the scenes, Hoover was intent on "containing" the most important civil rights leader of all. Starting in 1957, the FBI spied on Martin Luther King Jr. and other members of King's civil rights group, the Southern Christian Leadership Conference. The Bureau tried to give

King a bad name and reduce his influence. In 1976, Congress released a report about FBI activities concerning King. The report noted:

> From December 1963 until his death in 1968, Martin Luther King, Jr., was the target of an intensive campaign by the Federal Bureau of Investigation to "neutralize" him as an effective civil rights leader. . . . The FBI collected information about Dr. King's plans and activities through an extensive **surveillance** program, employing nearly every intelligence-gathering technique at the Bureau's disposal. . . . Attempts were made to prevent the publication of articles favorable to Dr. King and to find "friendly" news sources that would print unfavorable articles.

President Lyndon B. Johnson was a major supporter of civil rights, and Johnson used his influence to get important new civil rights laws enacted. Johnson also ordered Hoover to investigate the murders of three civil rights workers in Mississippi in 1964. Despite Hoover's initial resistance, the FBI targeted racial intimidation and violence in the South. A new COINTELPRO was able to disrupt the Ku Klux Klan and reduce its power.

This burned-out car belonged to three civil rights workers who were murdered near Philadelphia, Mississippi, in June 1964. FBI agents investigating the crime designated the case "MIBURN," for "Mississippi Burning."

A New Direction

By the early 1970s, however, many people were criticizing FBI operations. In 1971, secret documents were stolen from the FBI's office in Media, Pennsylvania. Some of the FBI's hidden activities came to light. Hoover stopped the COINTELPRO operations right away.

L. Patrick Gray became FBI director in 1972. Gray appointed the first female agents since the 1920s, but his tenure was short. A scandal forced him to resign in 1973.

Hoover died in 1972. President Richard Nixon appointed L. Patrick Gray to take Hoover's place. Gray was forced to resign amid scandal in April 1973. From April to June of that year, the FBI was led by William Ruckelshaus. Clarence Kelley replaced Ruckelshaus, serving as FBI director until 1978.

During these years, Congress examined the role of the FBI. Congressional investigations uncovered many abuses of power that were similar to the actions the Bureau had taken to discredit Martin Luther King Jr. The government decided that the FBI needed to be watched more closely. The Department of Justice gave the Bureau new guidelines—not just about its role, but for how it operated. The FBI was to focus less on domestic intelligence—such as spying on U.S. citizens—and more on real security issues and crime. It was to target white-collar (business) crime and keep pursuing the Mafia.

Changing Profile

With the help of the OCCSS and RICO laws, the FBI fought and won many battles against white-collar crime and organized crime. Agents in the 1970s began to use under-cover operations in their criminal work. They also worked more with law officers in other countries.

Even the profile of agents was changing.

WATERGATE

A huge political scandal hit the nation in 1972 and continued into 1974. In June 1972, police in Washington, D.C., arrested five men inside the Democratic National Committee headquarters. The men were photographing documents and had placed bugs in the building. The FBI was called in to investigate. The affair became known as "Watergate," after the Watergate hotel complex where the break-in took place.

Agents soon found themselves investigating high-level government officials working for President Richard M. Nixon. It turned out the burglars had been sent by officials from the Republican Party. But it was hard for the FBI to prove a connection between the burglars and government officials. While FBI agents worked to investigate the crime, White House officials were busy trying to hide the evidence.

L. Patrick Gray, the acting FBI director, became involved in the cover-up when he destroyed some White House documents. In 1973, Gray was forced to resign over the matter. Eventually, the ongoing investigation into Watergate exposed the role of top White House officials in the cover-up. In the end, even President Nixon was forced to resign.

The Watergate scandal reached the highest levels of the U.S. government. Among the officials forced from office by the scandal were acting FBI director L. Patrick Gray, Attorney General John Mitchell, top presidential advisers John Erlichman and H. R. Haldeman, and even President Richard M. Nixon.

Under Hoover, FBI agents were overwhelmingly white and male. After Hoover died, the FBI began to employ more women, African Americans, and Hispanics. The Bureau now has an office to promote diversity and equality. "Today, women in the FBI are supervisors, program managers, Unit Chiefs, Section Chiefs, Special Agents in Charge, and Executive Assistant Directors," Cassandra M. Chandler said in a 2005 speech in her role as the FBI's assistant director of the Office of Public Affairs. "Women in the FBI are vocal, powerful, and invaluable contributors."

FAST FACTS

In 1988, Judge Lucius D. Bunton ruled that the FBI discriminated against its Hispanic workers. The federal judge later ordered the FBI to change its system for promoting agents.

Cassandra M. Chandler became the highest-ranking African American woman in the FBI in December 2002, when she was appointed assistant director of the Office of Public Affairs and the FBI's national spokesperson. In 2005 she was named special agent in charge of the Norfolk (Virginia) Region. She retired from the FBI to pursue a private career in 2006.

6 Homeland Security: Bombings, 9/11, and Beyond

During the 1980s, the FBI expanded its work in several areas. Many investigations targeted illegal drugs and violent crime. The Intelligence Division expanded its work against foreign threats.

On April 19, 1995,
a massive truck bomb destroyed the
Alfred P. Murrah Federal Building in Oklahoma City, killing 168 people.
The FBI quickly traced the rented truck in which the bomb had been placed
to a former soldier named Timothy McVeigh. McVeigh said he carried out
the bombing to punish the U.S. government.

FRAUD IN THE 21ST CENTURY

Fraud means deceiving people, and most white-collar crime involves fraud. From its early days, the FBI has tackled white-collar crime. But criminals keep finding more ways to trick people out of their money. The FBI investigates fraud, or scams, in every area of life.

Some of the earliest scams involved land fraud or getting people to invest money in fake ventures. Con artists often used the telephone to defraud people. Today, most fraud reported by individual victims is Internet-related. Identity theft is also common today—criminals pretend to be someone else to obtain money and benefits.

Many forms of fraud are hard to pin down. Agents have to be financial experts to detect some kinds of theft. Since the 1990s, the FBI has convicted many top executives of stealing from their own companies. Taxpayers' money disappears through fraud in government projects. Fraud in health care costs the United States billions of dollars every year.

Crimes involving mortgages (money borrowed to buy houses) boomed in 2007 and 2008. In June 2008, the FBI announced Operation Malicious Mortgage. In just a few months, the Bureau had arrested more than 400 people who were allegedly defrauding borrowers.

Going Undercover

The FBI also tackled **corruption**. Agents went undercover in Operation ABSCAM, which exposed politicians who were willing to use their power in exchange for money. From 1978 to 1980, FBI agents approached politicians, pretending they were working for a rich Arab man. The FBI set up a fake office in Washington, D.C., where members of Congress and other public officials were offered bribes. Twelve officials, including a senator and six congress-men, were convicted.

Operation GREYLORD again took agents under-cover. This time, the targets were corrupt lawyers and judges. FBI agents posed as lawyers and even as defendants in fake cases designed to catch corrupt officials. Between 1980 and 1991, Operation GREYLORD found more than 90 corrupt officials in the Illinois legal system.

New Problems, New Responses

In 1982, the government gave the FBI more powers to fight the rising tide of illegal drugs. The FBI busted a large drug ring in 1984 that used pizza parlors as a front for heroin dealing. The international operation involved members of the Mafia in the United States and in Italy. The bust, which came to be known as the "Pizza Connection," involved law enforcement officials from Italy, the New York Police Department, and the FBI.

FAST FACTS

The FBI took charge of security for the 1984 Olympics, held in Los Angeles, California. To prepare for the event, the agency created its Hostage Rescue Team in 1983. The team has since responded to many **hostage** situations.

In the United States, violent crime surged during the 1980s. The end of the Cold War in 1991 gave the FBI a chance to address this surge. Hundreds of agents were taken off foreign duties and started tackling violent crime at home.

Bad Times

The FBI endured difficult times in the early 1990s. In August 1992, the FBI's Hostage Rescue Team was called to Ruby Ridge, Idaho. There had been a shoot-out between U.S. marshals and a wanted man named Randy Weaver at Weaver's remote cabin. During the standoff that followed, an FBI sniper shot and killed Weaver's wife.

In early 1993, the FBI's Hostage Rescue Team was again deployed. In this case, members of a religious group, the Branch Davidians, were holed up inside their compound in Waco, Texas. In February, agents of the Bureau of Alcohol, Tobacco, and Firearms (ATF) had raided the compound to arrest the group's leader and search for illegal weapons. A gunfight ensued, during which four ATF agents were killed and 15 others wounded. The FBI quickly assumed command on the scene. But the Bureau's hostage unit was unable to negotiate a surrender. On April 19, after a 51-day standoff, the FBI tried to dislodge the Davidians with armored vehicles and tear gas. Instead, a fire broke out and quickly consumed the compound, killing about 80 men, women, and children. The FBI would contend that the Davidians had deliberately set the fire themselves, but many people did not believe that.

Fire engulfs the Branch Davidian compound in Waco, Texas, April 19, 1993. Nearly 80 members of the religious group died in the blaze, which erupted after the FBI tried to end an armed standoff. Many Americans were critical of the FBI's conduct in the matter.

Many people blamed the FBI for the bloodshed at Ruby Ridge and Waco. A *New York Times* headline on April 20, 1993, read:

> "Scores Die as Cult Compound Is Set Afire After
> FBI Sends in Tanks with Tear Gas."

Yet again, Congress investigated. In 1994, the FBI formed the Critical Incident Response Group to manage crisis situations.

Meanwhile, FBI director William Sessions was also in trouble. Sessions had become head of the FBI in 1987. Inside the Bureau, Sessions was criticized for using federal funds for personal expenses. An investigation by the Department of Justice found that Sessions had committed ethical violations. On July 19, 1993, President Bill Clinton fired him.

Bomb Plots

During the 1980s and 1990s, the FBI conducted investigations into a number of bombings. These included a series of package bombs whose victims included researchers and computer scientists. The unknown terrorist was dubbed the Unabomber. In 1996, the FBI caught the Unabomber, who turned out to be a reclusive former university professor named Theodore Kaczynski.

While living in this remote cabin in Montana, Theodore Kaczynski waged a violent campaign against modern technology, which he believed was taking away people's basic freedoms. For nearly 18 years, Kaczynski mailed or planted homemade bombs that killed 3 people and injured 23 others. He was caught in 1996, after the longest manhunt in FBI history.

New York City firefighters walk amid the rubble of the World Trade Center, which was destroyed in the terrorist attacks of September 11, 2001. In the aftermath of September 11, the FBI was given expanded powers to combat terrorism.

Another high-profile case was the 1993 bombing at the World Trade Center in New York City. In that case, a truck bomb was detonated in an underground garage, killing six people. A huge FBI investigation led to the capture of a group of Muslim extremists who had planned and carried out the bombing. In 1995, a huge truck bomb destroyed a federal government building in Oklahoma City and killed 168 people. The perpetrator in that case turned out to be an American extremist named Timothy McVeigh.

The FBI stepped up its surveillance of extremist groups. It became more and more concerned with the threat of terrorism. Under Director Louis J. Freeh, the FBI strengthened its ties with law enforcement agencies in other parts of the world.

Terrorist Strikes and Responses

On September 4, 2001, Robert S. Mueller III took over as FBI director. Just one week later, a terrible event brought sudden change to the nation and to the FBI. On

September 11, terrorists belonging to a Muslim extremist group called al-Qaeda flew two hijacked passenger planes into the World Trade Center in New York City and one plane into the Pentagon near Washington, D.C. A fourth hijacked plane crashed into a field in western Pennsylvania following a struggle between hijackers and the plane's passengers and crew. It is believed that the plane was headed for either the White House or the Capitol in Washington. In all, about 3,000 people were killed in the attacks.

After September 11, the FBI received new guidelines. In October 2001, Congress passed, and President George W. Bush signed into law, the USA Patriot Act. It sought to address the threat of terrorism. One of the ways

FIGHTING CRIME WITH SCIENCE AND TECHNOLOGY

Since 1932, the FBI Laboratory has been using science to help solve crimes. The lab has matched fingerprints and examined microscopic fibers. Agents have pieced together countless fragments from crime scenes, turning them into vital evidence. The 1980s and 1990s saw a huge leap forward in crime detection. Forensic science (science used in the law) has gained many new tools. These tools help the FBI identify criminals and prove cases.

One major break-through was DNA analysis. DNA is information carried in people's cells. It can be used to link a person to a crime or to identify missing persons. Today, FBI files contain several million DNA profiles as well as millions of fingerprint sets.

Computer power helped the FBI's Criminal Justice Information Services build a huge **database**. The system handles an average of 5.5 million queries every day. Data can be used to track down criminals in several ways. One method is link analysis. A computer can pull together all kinds of information—police records, photos, phone logs, and agents' notes—and see how it connects. The FBI also has a unit called the Computer Analysis and Response Team (CART). The team's experts pull all kinds of crucial evidence from criminals' computers.

it did this was by giving the FBI expanded powers to monitor Americans. Critics of the Patriot Act say it extends FBI powers too far.

In the wake of the September 11 attacks, the FBI has extended its counterterrorism work abroad to a greater degree than ever. In April 2008, Director Mueller said:

> We never know when a fragment of information uncovered in one country could unearth an entire network of terror in another. . . . The intelligence we seek often resides where our adversaries are based, not where we are based.

The FBI Today

Since 2005, the FBI has had a new division: the National Security Branch (NSB). The NSB is part of the U.S. intelligence community, which is coordinated by the Director of National Intelligence (DNI). The office of DNI was created to oversee all security and intelligence efforts in the United States.

The FBI's role in investigating and, more important, in preventing terrorism has been growing. As a 2006 article in the *New York Times* stated:

> The number of Joint Terrorism Task Forces, in which FBI agents collaborate with state and local agencies, has ballooned to 101, from 35. The number of intelligence analysts has doubled to 2,161, and the number of linguists has doubled to 1,371. And the FBI points out that there has been no new terrorist attack.

The old arguments about the FBI's intelligence gathering role are still alive, however. Some people remain uneasy about what the *New York Times* called "the dangers of uncontrolled domestic spying."

100 Years of the FBI

On July 26, 2008, the FBI celebrated 100 years of service to the United States. How has it changed over the years? How do those changes reflect bigger changes in the nation?

The Bureau was founded in 1908 to enforce federal laws. Since that time, it has developed a very different role. J. Edgar Hoover, for decades the head of the Bureau, turned the FBI into a powerful force. But in the course of its work, the FBI has often invaded people's privacy. It has also used its power to shape events. Recent fears about terrorism have allowed the FBI to expand its powers yet again. Americans want to be secure. They expect the FBI to help keep them safe. But the nation is still struggling to find a balance between protecting itself and protecting its freedoms. And, once again, the FBI finds itself at the center of the debate.

FAST FACTS

The FBI targets Internet or **cyber crimes** and crimes against children with a program known as the Innocent Images National Initiative (IINI). The operation began in 1995 to reduce child pornography on the Internet. The IINI team works nationwide and now has an international task force.

Preventing sexual predators from exploiting children by means of the Internet is one of the goals of the FBI's Innocent Images National Initiative.

CHRONOLOGY

1908: An unnamed force of special agents (later the FBI) is created in the Department of Justice.

1909: The force is named the Bureau of Investigation.

1910: The Mann Act is passed, making it illegal to transport women across state lines for immoral purposes.

1917: The United States enters World War I. J. Edgar Hoover starts work for the Department of Justice.

1919: The Motor Vehicle Theft Act gives Bureau agents more powers to pursue criminals across state lines. The General Intelligence Division (GID) is created.

1920: Thousands of suspected communists are rounded up by Bureau of Investigation and Bureau of Immigration officials in the Palmer Raids. Prohibition begins.

1921: J. Edgar Hoover becomes assistant director of the Bureau.

1923: Ku Klux Klan leader Edward Y. Clarke is charged under the Mann Act.

1924: J. Edgar Hoover becomes acting director of the Bureau. The Bureau's Fingerprints Division is created.

1925: Edwin C. Shanahan is the first Bureau agent killed in the line of duty.

1928: The Bureau opens a training school for new agents.

1932: The Bureau of Investigation is renamed the U.S. Bureau of Investigation. The Lindbergh baby is kidnapped in New Jersey. The Bureau's Crime Laboratory is established.

1933: The U.S. Bureau of Investigation becomes the Division of Investigation. Four lawmen are shot in the Kansas City Massacre.

1934: Clyde Barrow and Bonnie Parker are killed by police officers in Louisiana. John Dillinger is killed by federal agents in Chicago.

1935: The Division of Investigation is renamed the Federal Bureau of Investigation. The FBI National Academy is founded.

1936: Hoover begins a huge intelligence-gathering operation to collect information about suspected radicals.

1939: World War II begins.

1940: The Special Intelligence Service (SIS) is created to gather intelligence about fascist activity in South America.

1941: Japan attacks Pearl Harbor, Hawaii, on December 7, pulling the United States into World War II. The FBI rounds up resident aliens from Italy, Germany, and Japan.

1942: German saboteurs arrive by submarine on Long Island, New York, and in Florida.

1945: World War II ends. The FBI starts probing U.S. government employees.

1947: The House Committee on Un-American Activities (HUAC) begins a probe of the U.S. entertainment industry.

1950: The FBI arrests Ethel and Julius Rosenberg for espionage. The FBI's "Ten Most Wanted Fugitives" list begins.

1956: The FBI counterintelligence programs (COINTELPROs) begin.

1957: Mafia bosses are observed meeting in New York. Hoover creates the Top Hoodlum program. The FBI begins monitoring Martin Luther King Jr.

1963: President John F. Kennedy is assassinated in November.

1964: Three civil rights workers are murdered in Mississippi. The new FBI COINTELPRO targets racial violence in the South. President Lyndon Johnson issues a special order allowing Hoover to stay in office after age 70.

1968: Martin Luther King Jr. is assassinated in April. Senator Robert F. Kennedy is assassinated in June.

1969: The Omnibus Crime Control and Safe Streets (OCCSS) Act is passed.

1970: The Racketeer Influenced and Corrupt Organizations (RICO) law is passed.

1971: Hoover halts COINTELPROs.

1972: J. Edgar Hoover dies, ending nearly 50 years as director. The new FBI Academy opens in Quantico, Virginia. The Watergate break-in occurs.

1973: The FBI directorship changes several times following the Watergate cover-up.

1978: Operation ABSCAM starts targeting corrupt politicians.

1979: John D. Glover becomes the first African American to head an FBI field office, in Milwaukee.

1980: Operation GREYLORD targets corruption in the Illinois legal system.

1982: The FBI gains more jurisdiction over illegal drug violations.

1983: The Hostage Rescue Team is created.

1984: The National Center for the Analysis of Violent Crime (NCAVC) opens at the FBI Academy. The FBI busts a large international heroin-dealing operation.

1988: A federal judge rules that the FBI has been discriminating against Hispanics.

1991: The Cold War comes to an end.

1992: The Hostage Rescue Team shoots a fugitive's wife in Ruby Ridge, Idaho.

1993: A bomb set by Muslim extremists explodes at the World Trade Center in New York. Nearly 80 people die in a fire at a religious group's compound in Waco, Texas, during an FBI operation.

1994: The FBI's Critical Incident Response Group is formed.

1995: A bomb explodes on April 19 at a building in Oklahoma City, killing 168 people. Operation Innocent Images, targeting Internet-based child pornography, is announced.

1996: The FBI catches the Unabomber, Theodore Kaczynski.

1999: Terrorist leader Osama bin Laden is placed on the FBI's "Ten Most Wanted" list.

2000: The FBI Laboratory starts the National Missing Person DNA Database (NMPDD).

2001: Terrorists attack the World Trade Center in New York and the Pentagon near Washington, D.C., on September 11. The Patriot Act is passed. FBI Headquarters is reorganized under new guidelines.

2005: The FBI's National Security Branch is created.

2008: More than 400 people are arrested in Operation Malicious Mortgage. The FBI celebrates its 100th anniversary on July 26.

GLOSSARY

activist — a person who takes action in support of one side of an issue, especially in politics.

alien — a person who is not a citizen of the country he or she is living in.

blacklist — to create or use a list of people who are barred from some activity.

conspiracy — a plot or an agreement to act together.

corruption — dishonest or immoral behavior, especially by public officials.

counterintelligence — an activity by one agency that aims to block another agency from getting information. Counter-intelligence is also used to deceive enemies with false information and to prevent acts of sabotage.

cyber crime — a crime committed in a computer network or by using computer technology.

database — a large, organized collection of information stored in a computer system.

double agent — a person who appears to work for one side while actually working for or giving information to an enemy.

espionage — the act of spying to steal government secrets.

evidence — material used to uncover truth or to prove guilt in a crime.

fascist — a person who believes in complete government control of society.

fugitive — a person who is running away, especially someone who is trying to escape from the law.

hostage — a person who is held captive to force demands to be met or in exchange for money.

intelligence — information collected about possible threats or enemies.

Ku Klux Klan — a secret organization using violence, intimidation, and terrorism to threaten or harm African Americans, Jews, and other racial or religious minorities.

money laundering — the act of processing money that has been acquired illegally in order to conceal where it came from (for example, by investing the money in a legitimate business).

radical — a person who wants to make extreme changes in society.

sabotage — the destruction of property, such as a factory or railroad, by a civilian in order to damage a country's war effort.

subversive — designed or intended to undermine a society or cause the overthrow of a government.

surveillance — the close and often secret monitoring of a person and his or her activities.

undercover — disguised in order to gain entry into criminal circles.

wiretap — a device that cuts in on a telephone wire to enable people to listen to conversations held on the line.

FURTHER READING

Burgan, Michael. *Spying and the Cold War* (On the Front Line). Chicago: Raintree, 2005.

De Capua, Sarah. *The FBI* (Cornerstones of Freedom). New York: Children's Press, 2007.

Holden, Henry M. *FBI 100 Years: An Unofficial History*. Minneapolis: Zenith Press, 2008.

Streissguth, Thomas. *J. Edgar Hoover: Powerful FBI Director* (Historical American Biographies). Berkeley Heights, NJ: Enslow, 2002.

Theoharis, Athan G. (editor). *The FBI: A Comprehensive Reference Guide*. New York: Checkmark Books, 2000.

Wachtel, Alan. *The FBI's Most Wanted* (The FBI Story). Broomall, PA: Mason Crest Publishers, 2009.

INTERNET RESOURCES

http://www.coldwar.org/museum/museum_features.html
Click on the timeline tabs at the bottom of the Cold War
Museum's features page to find in-depth information
about many aspects of the Cold War.

http://www.fbi.gov/fbihistory.htm
History section of the official FBI Web site leads to many
historical items. Headline articles and archives as well as
photos and radio excerpts can all be accessed from this page.

http://www.fbi.gov/fbikids.htm
The kids' page of the official FBI Web site offers activities and
information for 6th- to 12th-grade students.

http://www.usdoj.gov/
Official Web site of the U.S. Department of Justice.

The Web sites mentioned in this book were active at the time of
publication. The publisher is not responsible for Web sites that have
changed their addresses or discontinued operation since the date of
publication. The publisher will review and update the Web site
addresses each time the book is reprinted.

NOTES

Chapter 1

p. 7: "At last we have . . ." W. H. Drane Lester, "FBI," *The Investigator*, September 1935, **www.fbi.gov/libref/historic/fbiseal/fbiseal.htm.**

p. 9: "To protect and defend . . ." Our Mission, Federal Bureau of Investigation, **www.fbi.gov/quickfacts.htm.**

Chapter 2

p. 13: "It became impossible . . ." Charles J. Bonaparte, letter to Theodore Roosevelt, January 14, 1909, Historical Documents from the Bureau's Founding, Federal Bureau of Investigation, **www.fbi.gov/libref/historic/history/historic_doc/doc1909jan.htm.**

p. 13: "investigations under the Department . . ." Founding Order, July 26, 1908, Historical Documents from the Bureau's Founding, Federal Bureau of Investigation, **www.fbi.gov/libref/historic/history/historic_doc/foundingorder.htm.**

p. 14: "the globalization of crime . . ." Robert Mueller, quoted in "The FBI's International Presence," Federal Bureau of Investigation, **www.fbi.gov/contact/legat/legat.htm.**

p. 18: "Revolution Smashed . . ." Athan G. Theoharis (ed.), *The FBI: A Comprehensive Reference Guide* (New York: Checkmark Books, 2000), p. 9.

Chapter 3

p. 20: "political or other opinions . . ." Harlan F. Stone, quoted in Theoharis, *The FBI*, p. 11.

p. 22: "The Agents of the Bureau . . ." J. Edgar Hoover, remarks prepared for the Attorney General, 1925, "History of the FBI, Lawless Years: 1921–1933," Federal Bureau of Investigation, **www.fbi.gov/libref/historic/history/lawless.htm.**

p. 24: "He was hiding out . . ." John Fox, interviewed on *FBI 100: A Closer Look*, June 6, 2008, ABC Radio Networks.

Chapter 4

p. 32: "Every complaint in this . . ." J. Edgar Hoover, memo to Attorney General Francis Biddle. Quoted in Asian American Studies Institute at the University of Connecticut, Japanese American Internment Resource Library, **http://asianamerican.uconn.edu/jarl.htm.**

p. 33: "an invasion has been perpetuated . . ." Franklin D. Roosevelt, Presidential Proclamation 2525, Washington, D.C., December 7, 1941.

p. 35: "appear to be under control . . ." FBI memorandum, February 1943, quoted in Henry M. Holden, *FBI 100 Years: An Unofficial History* (Minneapolis: Zenith Press, 2008), p. 89.

p. 36: "In my opinion . . ." Joseph McCarthy, speech at the Women's Republican Club, Wheeling, West Virginia, February 9, 1950.

Chapter 5

p. 39: "did signal to the FBI . . ." John Fox, interviewed on *FBI 100: A Closer Look*, November 2, 2007, ABC Radio Networks.

p. 43: "From December 1963 until . . ." United States Senate, *Final Report of the Select Committee to Study Governmental Operations with Respect to Intelligence Activities.*

p. 46: "Today, women in the FBI . . ." Cassandra M. Chandler, speech at FBI's Criminal Justice Information Services Division, Clarksburg, West Virginia, March 30, 2005.

Chapter 6

p. 51: "Scores Die as Cult Compound . . ." Sam Howe Verhovek, "Scores Die as Cult Compound Is Set Afire After FBI Sends in Tanks with Tear Gas," *New York Times*, April 20, 1993.

p. 54: "We never know when . . ." Robert Mueller, speech at Chatham House, London, England, April 7, 2008.

p. 54: "The number . . ." Scott Shane and Lowell Bergman, "F.B.I. Struggling to Reinvent Itself to Fight Terror, *New York Times*, October 10, 2006.

p. 54: "the dangers of . . ." Ibid.

INDEX

About the Author

Sabrina Crewe is an editor of children's educational books. She has edited many series of social studies and science books and is the author or co-author of 50 titles, including two in this series.